Leave me to my thoughts

By: Antionette Barnes

Copyright © 2023 Antionette Barnes All rights reserved

The characters and events portrayed in this book are fictitious. Any similarity to real persons, living or dead, is coincidental and not intended by the author.

No part of this book may be reproduced, or stored in a retrieval system, or transmitted in any form or by any means, electronic, mechanical, photocopying, recording, or otherwise, without express written permission of the publisher.

ISBN-13: 978-1-7370589-2-2

Printed in the United States of America

Table of contents:

- Something told me
- Being alone
- Forgive yourself
- Heads up
- Hold on
- Overthink
- Little things
- This
- Check-In with yourself
- Difference
- Sit with myself
- Reflect
- Reflection
- Voice
- I have the right
- Healing process
- Healing
- Working on myself
- Into your life
- I'm not trying to be
- Your future relationship
- Laugh
- Stay out
- Dream
- Inspire
- Lost myself
- On a break
- Wipe
- I'm in tears
- Bottled up
- Release my emotions
- You have the right to cry
- Manifest what I want
- Tried so hard not to
- Keep myself up

- ❖ Self-esteem
- ❖ Inner peace
- ❖ It
- ❖ Caution
- ❖ Woman's Cave
- ❖ Synonyms of free
- ❖ Do more
- ❖ Sleep
- ❖ Picture me
- ❖ Earn
- ❖ Wash away
- ❖ Free from my old self
- ❖ Virtual Hugs
- ❖ Self-Respect Blvd.
- ❖ Love yourself first
- ❖ You matter
- ❖ Learn from myself
- ❖ His
- ❖ Existing
- ❖ Sense
- ❖ Life partners
- ❖ Committed
- ❖ Mindset
- ❖ My purpose
- ❖ Constructive criticism
- ❖ Synonyms of feel
- ❖ Books by this author

I Create

I create my own happiness
For who knows how to make me happy better than me?
I create positive thoughts
For I am what I think

I create love in me
So, I can better spread love
I create a bond with myself
Learning my true self is important to me

I create my own affirmations
Speaking life to myself
Is important for my overall well-being
I create, I create, I create

I Attract

I attract what's for me
I attract positive vibes
I attract beautiful souls
I attract pleasure

I attract pure love
I attract authentic
I attract confident people
I attract my visions

For I only have room for what's positive
I'm destined for greatness
I will have what's best for me
I attract

...

Something told me

Something told me you weren't the one

Something told me to drop you

Leave you where you're at

Go to the nearest exit

Take it and leave

But I stayed

I passed the nearest exit

Well, I didn't go to it really

I hit that U-Turn real quick

Even though something told me….

Something told me that I was better off alone

Rather than being with you

That gut feeling kept getting bigger and bigger

As I got closer to you

I stayed anyway even though something told me

I had that gut feeling

Being alone

At first, I wasn't feeling it
At first, I thought I was cursed
In the beginning, I was a little confused
On why I seemed to always be alone

Until I came to a point in my life
Where I realized that
Being alone is part of my journey
Being alone is not so bad

I've been on a self-discovery journey while being alone
I've been more to myself while being alone
Being alone has taught me a lot
I value my alone time

Forgive yourself

You might be one of them
The ones who used to mistreat themselves
You blamed yourself
Because of other people

You allow other people to make
You feel guilty
To feel shameful
You were at war with yourself

You didn't know true love
Because you didn't show yourself that
You weren't really at peace
Because you didn't find your inner peace

Forgive yourself
Be kind to yourself
Work on 'you' for you
Forgive yourself

Heads up

Why should I have given you

A heads up

When I left up out of your life?

When you didn't give me

A heads up

When had you cheated on me?

Opportunities after opportunities

Is what you had

You ended up running out of opportunities with me

Our time together has expired

Forget a heads up

I'm not about that

Leaving you where you're at

With no warning

Is the message that you need

To know that I'm done with you

Hold on

Hold on!

What's going on here?

You mean to tell me

That I could have been felt this way?

Hold on!

So, there was true peace deep inside me

And for me to access it

I had to connect with myself

Hold on!

Hold on!

I have to hug myself

Tell myself that "I love you."

Overthink

Overthink
Where do I start?
I used to be bad at that
My mind used to create scenarios

I used to overthink
About how people feel about me
Overthink of what
People thought of me

Overthink
Thought too much on negative thoughts
It used to get to me
I was all up in my thoughts

I had to learn to focus
Be focused on positive thoughts
People's view of me is not my business
I'm in control of my thoughts

Little things

I appreciate the little things
They count in my life
I practice gratitude
Each and every day

I'm grateful for the things in my life
A smile will take me a long way
"I'm just checking on you."
Makes me feel like I matter

I embrace the little things
Small gifts that are just because
I can't go wrong with the little things
I see the difference in my life with little things

This

This is how it is
This is how it is going to be
You can't make me change my mind
There's no stopping me

I'm doing this for myself
My happiness matters to me
This is my life now
This solitude

Has brought me closer to myself
This heart of mine
Is getting more love from me
I speak affirmations daily

Check-in with yourself

You took care of other people
You made sure they were straight
You spent less time with yourself
Focusing on people outside of yourself

Why did you do that?
Why did you spend more time
On checking in with other people
Then with yourself?

Who checked up on you?
You matter too
Check-in with yourself
It's okay

Check-in with yourself
Your overall health matters too
Love yourself for yourself
Remember to check in with yourself

Difference

There's a difference between 'alone' and 'lonely'

There's a difference between 'love you' and 'I love you'

Don't get them confused

They must not be mistaken as the same

When I say I don't want you

You need to know that

Understand that

There's a difference between "I want you" and "I don't want you."

Sit with myself

It took me a while

To realize

That if I sit with myself

I will be able to listen to my inner thoughts

If I sit with myself

By myself

Then I can talk to myself

I can be at peace

There is a silence

When I sit with myself

But that silence is beautiful

That silence is peaceful

After I sit with myself

I feel a calmness

A peace of mind

It's beautiful

Reflect

Reflect on your life

How does that look to you?

How can it be better

Reflect on the changes

The changes that you need to make

To make your life better

Reflect on you

To see the true you

Are you the person who

You truly want to be?

Reflect on what you mean to you

How much do you love yourself?

Reflect on your thoughts

What kind of thoughts do you think?

How do they better serve you?

Be a better person for you

Reflection

I was a reflection of you

Did you know that?

How you treated me

Was how I treated you

Did you see the reflection

Of my actions?

I started treating myself unkindly

Because you didn't always treat me right

I had to pull away from you

I no longer wanted to be a reflection of you

I deserve true love

With you, it just wasn't there

Voice

I found my voice

It took me a while

My silence has been turned into words

My fears of speaking

Has disappeared

My voice will be heard

You can guarantee that

I was once ashamed of my voice

Now, I embrace it

I practice speaking clearly

My words will be understood

I have the right to voice my opinions

I have the right

I have the right to voice my opinion

My voice matters too

Keeping it in won't help me

I tried that before

It didn't work

My voice will be heard

I will be understood

I have the right to express myself

My days of

Keeping it all in is over

Check out this new me

I have the right to be me

Healing process

I'm going through this healing process alone
I don't really know what I'm doing
How is this healing process supposed to go?
How long will it take?

This healing process is worth it
I must say
I will figure it out eventually
I'm sure of it

If I truly want to connect with myself
I will have to go through
Some kind of healing process
I will be a different person when I come out

Healing

I can feel myself healing

I've learned to sit with myself

With healing means making peace with my past

With healing means making peace with myself

Healing the wounds that were caused on me

Caused by myself

Caused by the world

This healing takes time

Healing through meditation

Healing in silence

This is what's best for me

I will be whole again

Working on myself

I separated myself away from the world
I felt like that was the best thing to do
I have to find myself
Well, rediscover myself

I'm working on myself
For myself
This is what I have to do alone
In solitude

Working on myself
Stopped talking to people with no warning
Well, I only had associates
Working on myself

Bettering myself
Working on myself
Focusing on myself
Learning myself

Into your life

I miss you

I wish things would have started off

Different with us

Then maybe things would have

Ended up different than they did

You were a great man

But I will not enter

Into your life

No time soon

I know you want me in your life

Know that when people come into your life

That an expiration date comes with them

I'm not trying to be

At first, I admit

That I wanted to be

The woman for you

I wanted to be your girlfriend

Then suddenly,

I came to my senses

Now, I'm not trying to be

The one for you

I'm not trying to be

Someone who I'm not

I'm not trying to be

Someone who I'm not comfortable being

Your future relationship

I had a dream of your future relationship

Two to be exact

What started off as my dreams

Became your reality

I had those dreams back to back

In one night

I hit you up

And you were surprised

That I dreamed of you

And the contents of the dream

You made the dream come true

You made her your girlfriend

I took that as a sign

To leave you alone

I wished you well in your new relationship

Then I eventually left up out your life

Laugh

I had to re-learn how to do that
For a while, I wasn't doing it
I was forging a laugh here and there
I wonder if anyone could tell

My fake laugh from my real laugh
There were multiple times in my life
Where I was down and really low
Low self-esteem kept my real laugh in

With depression, it was easy to forge a fake laugh
Who am I kidding?
Fake laugh or real laugh
It was hard to laugh

Now, I'm at a place in my life
Where I love to laugh
It's comes naturally to me now
Laugh to keep myself up

Stay out

Now that I got you out of my life

I want you to stay out

This time it's for good

I mean that

Stay out

Stay away

I'm good without you

I don't see the value

That we were doing

To each other's life

Stay out

Unless you changed

Changed only for the better

I will not take you back into my life

Stay out

I only want good vibes from strong-minded people around me

Dream

If I dream it,

It will come true

If I dream it,

I should believe it

I'm the type of person

Who loves to dream

I'm the type of person

Who loves to act on my thoughts

If I dream it,

I should manifest it

If I dream it,

I should make it my reality

Inspire

Inspire

Such a beautiful word

Who do you inspire?

Do you inspire yourself?

Think of all of the people

Who you can inspire

You can inspire with your words alone

You can inspire with your actions alone

Inspire

Motivate

Encourage

Be a positive influence in someone's life

You can inspire people to have courage

You can inspire people to love themselves

Inspire with your confidence

Inspire with your honesty

Lost myself

Once upon a time,

I knew myself

Well, I knew myself well enough

Even though I had low self-esteem

Somewhere throughout my life

I lost myself

Almost completely

Don't ask me how that came about

Lost myself

I was in the lost and found

A portion of my life

Not even realizing it

Until one day came

And I felt like

I had to re-evaluate my life

That's when things started falling into place

On a break

I'm on a break right now

I'm on a journey

Of bettering myself

Of finding myself

I'm on a break

On relationships

I have to make sure

That I'm the one who someone is manifesting

I'm on a break

I'm not sure how long this break will be

I'm on a break

From a lot of things and a lot of people

Wipe

I wish that I can wipe you from my mind

Then that way

I can wipe you out of my system

There is no more room

Here in my life

For you

Not anymore

I wish I can wipe you away

Out of my life completely

You're taking up room

In my head

I need that space for new information

Or new people

I need to wipe you from my entire system

Just wipe you away

I want to forget you

I'm in tears

I'm in tears
Because I turned to
A new chapter in my book
I'm a better me

I'm in tears
Because I finally
Decided to let go of the past
I had to do it for me

I'm in tears
Because I had to let go
Of all my emotions
They were all bottled in

I'm in tears
Because I never felt this way before
I can say this with joy and love in my heart
I'm loving this new chapter in my life

Bottled up

My emotions were everywhere
But they were everywhere inside of me
I wouldn't let them out
They were all bottled up

I had no outlet
I had no one to talk to
I was all alone
They were all bottled up

I didn't know how to express myself
I was afraid to share my emotions
I didn't think they matter
They were all bottled up

I was screaming on the inside
Hoping someone heard me
Bottled up
I kept my emotions all bottled up

Release my emotions

I had to find ways to release my emotions
It wasn't healthy to keep them bottled in
I had learned to just cry
Cry them all out

Release my emotions
All of them
I wanted to feel better
I didn't want those emotions in no more

Release my emotions
I had to tell myself
It was okay to cry
I gave myself permission to

Release my emotions
Release all of them
When I did, I felt better
I felt so much better

You have the right to cry

Baby girl, don't hold them in
Let them out
Don't be afraid to release them
You have the right to cry

Young man, you have the right to cry
It's not healthy to keep them in
You matter too
Release them

You have the right to cry
You have the right to express yourself
So, tell yourself that
Even if you have to do it in solitude

You have the right to cry
Until you can't cry anymore
Your feelings matter too
It's okay to cry

Manifest what I want

I had learned

About a thing called manifest

I've been learning how this thing goes

How can I manifest what I want?

Different techniques

Trying to see what I want

Manifest what I want

Now, I know how to do it

I have the power to

With clear intentions

I can manifest what I want

And I do mean clear

With great focus

I can manifest what I want

Do it alone

Keep my thoughts on my intentions

Tried so hard not to

Tried so hard not to
Say anything
I was trying to keep it in
As much as I could

Tried so hard not to
Spill what had a lid on it
Keeping this all in
Is really hard

But I know I have to
Keep the lid on it
Tried so hard not to
Exposed what I'm manifesting

Keep it in
Keep it to myself
Mouth shut
Good news waiting to be shared

Keep myself up

I have zero time for games
The same with that petty stuff
I'm on a whole new level
A higher up level

I'm doing things for me
I have to keep myself up
Keep me in a good mood
Keep myself vibrating high

Keep myself up
I can do that
Keep myself up
What's the problem with that

Having confidence in myself
Speaking affirmations
Giving myself hugs
Loving every part of me

Self-esteem

You are not alone
A lot of us used to experience this
Most of us might still be going through this
This is something that's hard to overcome

Self-esteem can have people feeling low
Self-esteem can keep a person down
Self-esteem can make a person feel worthless
Only if their self-esteem is low

Get off of Low Self-Esteem Blvd.
Get onto Confidence In Myself Rd.
Turn into I Am Worthy neighborhood
There you will surely find yourself

Inner peace

My inner peace got me so calm
Sitting here in my own world
I just want to be left alone
I'm so at peace by myself

I should have been found my inner peace
This inner peace got me so relaxed
I'm loving myself more and more
I'm spending more and more time by myself

I can't go wrong with my inner peace
I embrace my inner peace
My inner peace got me so calm
My inner peace got me so relaxed

It

It doesn't matter
What people say about you
It doesn't matter
How others feel about you

It is none of your business
It is theirs
How someone feels about you
Is a reflection of how they see themselves

How someone thinks of you
Tells a lot about them
It is your job
To take care of yourself

It is your job
To see yourself for who you really are
It is up to you
To not let others get to you

Caution

When I come out of this state of solitude

I will be a new me

A better me

So, don't be alarmed

When I handle things with caution

This new attitude of mines

Comes with the better me

Caution

I will be showing love with caution

I will be more alert

Caution

When I first step out of this solitude state

I will love with caution

There is a lot of growth that I have to gain

Therefore, stepping out with caution

Will be beneficial to me

Woman's cave

This is my woman's cave
Where I can truly be myself
Where I can find myself
Alone time me, please

This is my woman's cave
Where I can truly relax
Sink deeper into my peace
I'm in my own world

This is my woman's cave
Where I can let it all go
Where I can direct my attention to "me"
This is my safe haven

Synonyms of free

What other ways can I tell you
To set free of what's not serving you?
You can do it without charge
As an independent person

Release your grip
For it is not for you
Detached from old habits
Unsecure the lid of negative feelings

Relax, it will all be okay
Once you untie yourself
From the string that's bounding you to insecurities
You are meant to have the freedom to be your true self

Do more

I wasn't satisfied with my life
I felt like I wasn't doing enough
So, I decided to do more
I just had to do more

I didn't feel complete
I wasn't complete
I have come to the conclusion
That I have to find out what I love

So, I can do more of it
Do more of what make me a better person
Do more of what make me laugh
Do more of what keep me mentally stable

Sleep

It comes so easy to me now

I sleep so peacefully

I sleep so good

I go to sleep by myself

This single life

Have me going to sleep alone

That's cool

I love it

No more sleep lost

No more nights of finding it hard to sleep

I cherish my alone time

while I'm asleep

Picture Me

Can you picture me

Happy in love

With the one who is for me?

I can

Picture me

Living out all of my dreams

The ones that I manifested

I know I am

Destine for greatness

I'm destined for greatness

There's greatness inside of me

It's time to bring it out

Picture me

Just picture me

Bettering myself

Living in my purpose

Earn

Don't let anybody in easily

Make them earn their right

Their right

To have access to you

Let them know

They will have to earn

Your time

They will have to earn

Your love

Don't just give them up for free

You are not for free

Make them earn you

Let yourself know that

You are somebody

You are somebody worth loving

Make them earn their way to you

Wash Away

I wish I can wash away

These feelings I have for you

But they're still

Floating around

I want to wash away

Those kisses of yours

But I still

Feel your lips on mines

Wash away

Just go away

I want to wash away your touches

Your gentle touches

Those thoughts of you

Are still lingering around

Here in my personal world

It's taking a lot to get you out of my system

Free From My Old Self

The old me is what the new me should have been

I came a long way

From where I started

I know I have a long way to go

I used to always wanted to be

Free from my old self

I wasn't satisfied with my old self

I wanted to be somebody other than myself

Free from my old self

Free from those negative thoughts in my mind

Free from my old self

I had no confidence in myself

Virtual hugs

When I say I miss him so much,
I mean that
When I send these hugs to him
Will he be able to feel them?

These are my virtual hugs
From me to him
When I send them
I imagine myself hugging him

Do you feel my virtual hugs?
You are so out of reach
I love intimacy on another level
And you used to always provide just that

How can I find out
That you received my virtual hugs?
These virtual hugs
Are all that I have of feeling your love

Self-Respect Blvd.

I took myself off of 'War with Myself Blvd.'

I moved away

I moved far away

I moved down onto "Re-evaluate St.'

Where I saw the intersection of

'Self-Respect Blvd.' and 'Self-Doubt Ave.'

I took the road

That was far away from 'War with Myself Ave.'

That's how I ended up

On 'Self-Respect Blvd.'

I love it here

I'm loving myself more

This is my permanent address

There is no moving from here

I made peace with myself

Here on 'Self-Respect Blvd.'

Love yourself first

Don't worry about what people say about you

Don't worry about how they feel about you

Do you

Love you

Love yourself first

So, you can experience love firsthand

Love yourself first

So, you can know not to settle for less

Put yourself first

Don't forget about you

Take wonderful care of you

Then people will know that you don't put up with anything

Love yourself first

So, that you can spread unconditional love

Love yourself first

So, the right love will find you

You matter

No matter how much you think you don't

No matter how much you feel that you don't

No matter what people say,

You matter

Know that you matter

Believe that you matter

Feel that you matter

Because believe me

You do matter

At times, it might not feel like it

That's okay

Tell yourself "I matter"

Feel it

Believe it

You should matter to yourself also

I know that you matter and you should know that too

Learn from myself

I have a lot to learn

I have a lot of wisdom to take in

Why not learn from myself?

Why not look deep within me?

Learn from myself

Ask myself deep and meaningful questions

Spend more time alone

So, that I can have more time with my thoughts

Learn from myself

So, I can learn more about myself

Self-teach myself

Be my own teacher

Learn from myself

Have patience with myself

Get the knowledge from within

Make myself a more knowledgeable person

His

His face

His scent

His voice

Are all about to fade away

His laugh

His touch

His stare

Are all leaving my mind

His warm hugs

His soft kisses

His words of inspiration

Are memories I want to keep

Make them my reality again

Back in each other's lives

Is he my twin flame?

I miss 'his' everything

Existing

All my life I have been doing this

Not even realizing it

You may ask

How could I not know?

No one told me

I thought existing was the same thing as living

Until I truly opened my eyes

Opened my eyes and my mind to different ways of thinking

I was existing

Not thinking that there were much more to my life

Existing

Not truly living

I was doing the same old same old

That's what I call existing

Not taking vacations

Not taking risks

Growth

I thank God for this
I thank myself for this
I went through a lot of trails
And not just once

I hit a level of maturity
That I will not come down from
I hit growth in my mindset
I changed up the way I think

With this growth
Comes a new me
I had to liberate myself
From my old ways

It was a really difficult journey
To come to this level of growth
I'm so glad that I'm here
Thank God for growth and maturity

Sense

There was a 'sense' that I had to leave him alone
I thought that maybe
He was blocking what was meant for me
Glad that I did

I always have a feeling of 'sense'
There's always a 'sense'
That I should or I shouldn't
Maybe it's my intuition

There's a part of me
Saying "Don't do it."
Then there's a part of me
Saying "Do it."

Having a 'sense'
Is my way of knowing
If I go against that 'sense'
It will just get bigger and bigger

Life Partners

I don't want a one-time fling

I don't want a "Maybe I'll be with you forever."

I want a sure thing

Let's make this forever

Life partners

Let's make each other a better person

A better version of ourselves

I never been with somebody

Who I felt a chemistry with

I never had a bond with anyone

I mostly always felt lonely

Even while being with people

Life partners

What's the true meaning of it?

I want love

I want unconditional love

Committed

I am so committed right now
At this point in my life
There is no turning back
That is not an option

I am committed to myself
Betraying myself is not an option
I am committed to my journey
I am trusting the process of the unknown journey

I am
Committed to bettering myself
Committed to discovering my true self
Committed to manifesting the life I deserve

Mindset

I must admit

That I came along way

From where I used to be

That point in my life is over

I decided that I had to elevate

I had to elevate my life

On so many levels

So, I started with my mindset

I had a poor mindset

That mindset kept me at a low-vibrational state

Now, my mindset is stronger

No more low self-esteem

With this new mindset,

I learned to have confidence in myself

I learned to love myself

I learned to appreciate being alone

My purpose

What's my purpose here?

Why did I come here?

Don't mind me

I'm all in my head

Wondering

Questioning

How can I find my purpose?

Am I meant to find my purpose?

Just leave me to my thoughts

I'm trying to figure this out

Cause I really want to know

At times, I feel like I'm wasting time

I've been on this journey of self-discovery

Trying to discover my true self

Connect with my true self

So, I feel like I must find my purpose or destiny

Constructive criticism

I used to take this hard
I used to not be able to take it
Crying
Words used to pierce my heart

I didn't care if it was negative criticism
Or constructive criticism
I didn't want to hear it
Like "Why are you talking to me like this?"

The way a person said something to me
Was way more important than their words
Constructive criticism
I let it build me now

Words don't get to me now
Constructive criticism
I can take that now
I have room for improvements

Synonyms of feel

I really don't know how to feel about now
It's like I'm numb right now
There are no emotions to come out
So, how am I to express myself?

I've been alone most of my life
I'm going throughout life
With nobody to embrace
With nobody to caress me

I had let all of my emotions come out
Along time ago
Many times throughout my weeks
Now what is left?

How am I to feel about my lonely journey?
I'm so numb to this
I'm going through this experience alone
Maybe it's meant to be

Books By This Author:

- ❖ Poetry From The Heart

- ❖ Unlock What's Deep Inside: Affirmation Journal

- ❖ Numb to this single life: A collection of poems for all of the single folks

www.ingramcontent.com/pod-product-compliance
Lightning Source LLC
Chambersburg PA
CBHW071033080526
44587CB00015B/2605